HAMLYN

E S

OUT AND ABOUT

RAY ROWE

CONTENTS

Faces of the countryside	2
Be prepared	4
Dressed for the part	6
Taking the weight	8
On the right track	10
Finding north	12
Choosing your route	14
Reading the weather	16
Why landscapes are all different	18
Setting up camp	20
What makes an ideal campsite?	22
Safety first	24
A treasure hunt	26
Through the looking glass	28
Taking it further	30
Index	32

FACES OF THE COUNTRYSIDE

Take a look at the world around you. There is a·tremendous variety of country-side out there waiting to be enjoyed. As the human population grows, and more and more people are concentrated in towns and cities, the chance to escape into real countryside to find peace and tran-quillity, fresh air and wildlife, excitement and challenge, becomes ever more import-ant for many people.

No matter where you live, there are plenty of different kinds of landscape to explore, each with its attractions and each offering a home to different kinds of plants and animals.

mixed deciduous woods

conifer woods

On a spring day in temperate parts of the world, there can be few more delight-ful experiences than a walk in a deciduous woodland. With the songs of the birds echoing all around, and the scent of wild flowers filling the air, a woodland can be a most peaceful place. And, if you are very lucky, you might catch a glimpse of a shy deer or a foraging fox.

Maquis is the name given to a type of shrubby country which is found all around the Mediterranean. It develops after forests have been cleared, and cons-ists of a dense mixture of evergreen shrubs between 1 and 3 m (40 to 120 in) high.

maquis

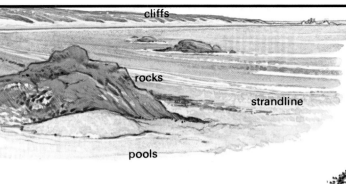

cliffs

rocks

strandline

pools

The seashore is always a good place to explore, especially where there are rock pools. These are often alive with sea creatures which either make their homes in the pools or which have been stranded there following a high tide. Always remember to check the tides so that you are never in danger of being cut off.

lakes

snow-capped mountains

moors

All animals and plants need water to be able to survive. And some, of course, live in or near freshwater areas, such as rivers, lakes, and ponds. There is always plenty to see here that is really fascinating, from the ever-busy waterbirds to the tall stands of bulrushes with their velvety seed heads.

desert

Mountains and moorlands offer solitude, challenge, and a real sense of being in the wild for those who have the skills and experience to venture among their remote valleys and peaks. Eagles may soar overhead while the heather carpets the land in a blaze of purple.

meadowland

Deserts may not look very inviting (indeed they are always risky places for people) but their plants and animals have become adapted to survive in such conditions. The spiny, fleshy spikes of cactuses conceal living reservoirs of moisture sucked up from deep beneath the sand, while some animals only venture out in the cold of the night.

BE PREPARED

If you're just going out into the garden, to a park, or just for a gentle ramble locally, you hardly need to prepare for much, other than wondering whether or not it's going to rain and what time you're expected back for dinner! On the other hand, the countryside can be demanding, so you ought to decide what sort of "out and about" you have in mind. Read a few books and magazines, watch some T.V. programmes, or join a local rambling, jogging, or orienteering club – you'll soon discover what particularly attracts you about being out and about.

You may have a dream that one day you'll be a famous mountaineer, tackling the north-west face of Everest in winter, or you might be content just to sit beside a local gravel pit identifying the birds on the water. But whatever the case, it's wiser (and more fun in the end) to be prepared.

Always make sure that someone knows where you're going and, if you're venturing into wild country, even if it's only for a few hours, you should never be alone. It's best always to be accompanied by a responsible adult who is experienced in the ways of the wild.

KEEPING FIT

Country walking is not only good fun – it's good for you! Regular exercise is essential if you're going to lead a healthy life, and is a really good back-up to almost every sport imaginable. But if you're planning to tackle any more demanding pursuit, such as rock climbing, fell walking, long-distance walking, or jogging, then it would be safer and more enjoyable if you were fit and properly warmed up *before* you go.

If you're lucky enough to have a gym or leisure centre nearby, then there'll quite likely be many other attractions which will also help you to get fit – from swimming to aerobics. On the other hand,

WARMING-UP EXERCISES

Knee bends
Stand with your feet a little apart. Bend your knees until you are almost in a squatting position. Then return to the standing position and repeat ten times.

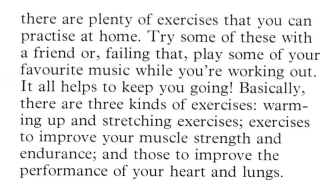

Ankle hug
Standing on one leg, bend the other back from the knee, clutching your ankle behind your back with both hands. Gently pull with your hands until the muscles at the front of your thighs feel taut. Do not pull too hard. Relax and repeat with the other leg.

there are plenty of exercises that you can practise at home. Try some of these with a friend or, failing that, play some of your favourite music while you're working out. It all helps to keep you going! Basically, there are three kinds of exercises: warming up and stretching exercises; exercises to improve your muscle strength and endurance; and those to improve the performance of your heart and lungs.

Step-ups

This is a good one to do if you have a low sturdy bench to step up on to. Using alternate legs, step up on to the bench and then down again. Continue until you begin to feel a little breathless.

Sit-ups

Lie on the floor with your hands behind your head, and your feet held down (ask a friend to help you). Trying to keep your legs as straight as you can, sit up until your head almost touches your knees. Lie back again. Repeat ten times. This is a good way to tighten your tummy muscles.

Wall stretch

This is to stretch the calf muscles and Achilles tendons (the muscle above the heel at the ankle). Stand facing the wall with your arms outstretched so that the flat of your hands are on the wall. Bend your arms, keeping your feet flat on the floor, until you are leaning forward and you can feel the muscles being stretched.

Thigh shift

Extend one leg backwards and the other forwards with the knee bent. Try again, using the other leg stretched backwards.

Even dogs need to be fit to accompany their owners into the Welsh hills.

Knee hug

Standing on one leg, bring the other one up in front of you, bending it at the knee, and clutching your knee with both hands. Gently pull it towards you until you can feel the muscles tightening. Do not pull too hard. You can also do this lying on your back. This exercise stretches the hamstrings.

DRESSED FOR THE PART

Your everyday clothes (tracksuits, jeans, T-shirt, and trainers, for example) are fine for casual outdoor wear in good weather. But if you're planning to venture far away from home then the clothes, including your footwear, that you wear or carry with you are very important.

Once again, it's a case of being prepared. Different kinds of walking, in different kinds of country, have different needs. And, of course, there's always the chance that the weather will change, especially in places like the British hills. For example, if you're out walking in February, it's quite possible that during the middle of the day, it may become quite warm. On the other hand, a blazing hot day in July at the foot of Ben Nevis may turn into a snow storm at the top.

Whatever you wear should be comfortable and should fit you well. It needs to keep you warm and dry (without making you sweaty!) when it's cold and wet, and cool when it's hot. You should also be able to change what you're wear-

ing to suit changing conditions. So the best idea is to wear several layers – you can always strip off bit by bit as and when necessary.

Trainers are ideal, unless you're walking somewhere that's likely to be very rough or wet. If trainers aren't suitable, there are three main types of footwear recommended, and these are described in detail below. Just try to remember that your boots or shoes have a lot of work to do. The soles should have a good grip to stop you skidding; they should protect the bottoms of your feet from any sharp stones and absorb the shock of perhaps thousands of footsteps. The uppers should be warm and waterproof for walking in cold, wet conditions, yet not too hot and sweaty; they should also help to protect the rest of your foot from damage and give support to the ankle if you're walking over uneven country. Above all, though, your boots or shoes should be as light as possible. It's hopeless trying to walk with great weights on the end of your legs!

These are called rock boots and are specially designed for rock climbers. The sole is made of a special sort of sticky rubber. These boots give a great grip on rocky walks.

These are rugged, heavy, leather mountain boots with a "Commando"-style rubber sole. They should be worn for very rough terrain and could be used in winter

when it's cold and wet The soles are very stiff – special spikes called "crampons" can be attached to them for climbing icy slopes.

These lightweight walking boots are just the job for general use. They're comfortable and flexible, but they still protect your feet and are reasonably waterproof. The sole is specially designed so that it doesn't clog with mud.

As much as 60 per cent of your body heat is lost through the top of your head. So, if it's cold wear a balaclava type hat. And, when it's hot and sunny, a hat will shade your eyes and help prevent heatstroke.

This kind of waterproof is often called a "shell garment" and will protect you from both wind and rain. Shell garments are often made from nylon for toughness, with a special backing for waterproofing. Of course, if your waterproof doesn't let the rain in, it may not let your sweat out either, but there is a range of good water-proofs that manage to do just that. Unfortunately, these tend to be horribly expensive.

If it's likely to be cold while you're out, take a woollen sweater or a good sweatshirt. Of course, if you have one, an anorak would be ideal. If you have the opportunity to buy a new one, go to a good outdoor shop for advice.

In very cold conditions, gloves or mittens are important. They now are made from many dif-ferent materials.

If it looks like rain, never wear jeans when out walking. They soak up water and soon become, heavy, clammy, and cold. There are all sorts of walking trousers available now in a variety of materials and colours, from heavyweight tweeds to light but windproof and quick-drying polycot-ton weaves.

Of course, shorts are very comfortable if it's hot, but be careful not to let your legs get sun-burned or, if you are somewhere where you might come across stinging plants or animals, then trousers may still be better. Waterproof trousers, made of the same material as your shell garment, are well worth taking with you on a long hike.

Some people hate wearing waterproofs. If you do, try gaters, which protect the bottom parts of your legs from wet, mud, and cuts.

Back to the boots again.

TAKING THE WEIGHT

You'll need some kind of rucksack for your spare clothing and any other bits and pieces of equipment that you might need. Again, these can be very expensive and there is a huge variety of different types and sizes. You can even buy a rucksack which has been tailored to fit your own back length. Your local outdoor shop will be able to give you good advice on the best kind to buy, but it is as well to do some research first so that, at least, you know what you will be using it for and how much you are likely to be carrying in it. Will you just need a spare pair of socks, a waterproof, a sweater, and perhaps a bar of chocolate, or will you be carrying all you need for a week's backpacking in the hills, where there are no shops (or people)?

It may be that you can carry everything you are likely to need in the pockets of your clothing – but don't forget, these may not be waterproof. Then there are small daypacks or waistpacks. Mountaineers and rock climbers need rucksacks to carry all their gear in, but they have to be designed so that they fit snugly to the body, do not make them top (or bottom) heavy and are unlikely to get snagged in rock crevices. A full expedition sack might

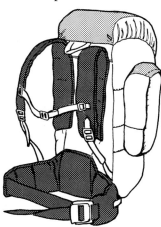

Left: *This popular rucksack has a harness system* (right) *which can be adjusted easily to fit the wearer's build comfortably.*

CHECKLIST
Remember to pack your rucksack with the heavier items at the top, especially for a longer expedition. So, starting from the bottom, you might include the following equipment:

- *sleeping bag and insulated mat*
- *emergency bag*
- *small first-aid kit*
- *extra warm clothing (if it is likely to become colder) or sunhat and shorts, for example*
- *waterproof clothing*
- *spare food*
- *cooking stove, pots, and pans (lightweight)*
- *whistle*
- *torch*
- *water and/or other drinks*
- *waterproof matches and spare fuel for stove*
- *lightweight tent*

There are other items you can add to suit your own needs, but try not to carry more than you need. Always remember to pack things so that you can get at them easily.

For a day's walk in the countryside, or even into wilder country, a full-size rucksack is likely to be too big. A smaller, lighter, but equally comfortable daypack is a much better bet.

have a pocket at the bottom, a main compartment, a pocket on the lid, and various pockets around the sides which may or may not be removeable. Sometimes, they also have special straps and loops for carrying things like ice axes.

Whatever kind of rucksack you're using, and whatever it's made from, it's not going to be 100 per cent waterproof, mainly because of the stitching. So, anything that you want to keep dry, such as spare clothing, should be kept in a plastic bag. Some people even line the whole of the inside of the sack with plastic bags.

You should also think about how you pack your rucksack. Obviously, things that you are likely to need quickly should be accessible but, on the other hand, it is a good idea to pack heavy things at the top, provided the items at the bottom will not get squashed. It is a good idea to practise packing your rucksack at home before you go to decide how heavy things are and how easy it is to get at the various bits of equipment. There's nothing worse than packing up everything you think you'll need, only to find you can't lift the sack – or stopping for lunch and having to take everything out of the pack to get at your sandwiches.

DON'T FORGET!

Sunglasses or a sunvisor are useful when the sun is dazzling. The polaroid type are the best.

A whistle can be used to give an emergency signal if you're in difficulty. Six blasts on it are the recognized distress signal.

A small torch is essential if you're out after dark.

Never go anywhere off the beaten track without a map and compass and without knowing how to use them. Make sure, too, that you have bought an accurate compass.

HOT AND DRY

Whenever it's hot and dry, always carry extra water with you. Even if it's cold, you might get thirsty. The aluminium 1 l (2 pt) bottles, obtainable in outdoor shops, are excellent.

When you sweat, your body loses salt, and if you lose a lot you can become ill. Salt tablets are the handy answer.

A sunhat will shade your eyes and help to keep your whole body cooler.

A sun barrier cream is worth carrying. Sunburn is pretty painful – and looks awful!

ON THE RIGHT TRACK

The minds of animals, including humans, are quite remarkable. Some birds, for example, newly emerged from the nest in one part of the world, are able to fly to another part of the world, thousands of kilometres away, where they might spend the winter. And all this without a map! It's thought that some birds, such as homing pigeons, even have a kind of built-in magnetic compass.

We're pretty good at finding our way around as well. Just think how many journeys you make without a map, simply because you've done the journey before, and you can remember the clues and the landmarks. Think of a journey that you know well, and then write down all the landmarks on that journey – road junctions, shops, a church, a factory, a special tree, and so on.

But, if you're going to strike out into unknown territory, you should have a map and compass and know how to use them. There are various points to remember about maps. Most important of all, they use different scales. For example, 1 km on the ground might be represented by 2 cm on the map. This is called a 1:50,000 scale and is a good one to use for walking. (A map worked out in inches and miles works in the same way.) A 1:25,000 scale map will show you even more detail. Most maps are arranged so that due north on the ground (geographic) is exactly to the top of the map. Maps indicate the height of the land by lines which show areas of equal height – these are called contour lines. They also use symbols to represent buildings, including churches and post offices; roads, railways, rivers, and lakes; car parks; woodland; crags; boggy ground and so on.

A magnetic compass is an instrument in which a pointer is pivoted on a fine point (and often damped by some kind of liquid) so that it can turn freely over a scale divided up into 360 degrees. One

end of the pointer, often coloured red, will always point to the Earth's magnetic north pole (in the northern hemisphere). Using a map and compass together, you can find your way around in places you don't know.

A good kind of compass to have is the "Silva" type. It comes with full instructions and you should read these and practise at home or in the park.

Triangulation (see diagram on page 12) can be worked out using a compass. Let's have a go.

Imagine you are on a footpath which you can see marked on the map, but you don't know how far along it you are. Choose a landmark in the distance, such as a mountain top or a church, that you can recognize on the map. Line up your compass with the landmark and turn the dial until the pointer lies north–south in the north–south rules on the compass. Next, place the compass on the map with

one edge on the landmark symbol. Align the edge of the compass, so that the north–south rules on the dial are in line with north–south on the map. The point where the edge of the compass crosses your path is how far along it you are. You can confirm this with one or more readings. But don't forget that magnetic north and geographic north are not the same (*see page 13*).

FINDING NORTH

You must be able to use a map and compass properly if you are to venture into unknown or remote country. They can help you to work out exactly where you are and also to plot your route.

It is not always easy to relate what you see on the map to the countryside that you see around you. Firstly, it is a good idea to hold your map in such a way that the north on the map is in line with north on the ground. You can do this accurately with a compass or roughly by the position of the sun.

Lay the map out on the ground and line up the compass on it so that the 0° to 180° line of the compass is in line with magnetic north–south. Then turn the map so that magnetic north–south lines up with the north–south of the compass needle. On the facing page, you can see how to find north using the sun and a wristwatch.

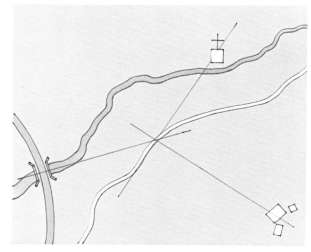

Triangulation can help you plot your position accurately.

Another useful way of setting the map and finding north at the same time (without using a compass) is to look for a feature on the ground, such as a railway

---

THE SILVA COMPASS

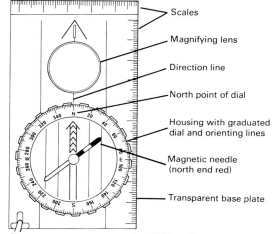

- Scales
- Magnifying lens
- Direction line
- North point of dial
- Housing with graduated dial and orienting lines
- Magnetic needle (north end red)
- Transparent base plate

For most purposes, the "Silva" type compass is the best to buy. It is light to carry and accurate to about 1°. There are various kinds, ranging from simple and quite cheap versions, to more sophisticated and expensive ones. The basic compass consists of a transparent plastic base (marked with scales and a direction line) and a liquid-filled section containing the magnetic needle in which the red end points to magnetic north.

Taking a bearing

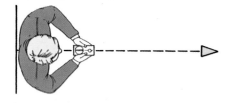

To take a bearing, hold the compass in front of you, so that the direction line points accurately at the object. Turn the housing of the compass so that the red end of the compass needle points to zero on the scale. The bearing of the object can be read off from the point where the direction line meets the scale on the compass.

Reading a bearing

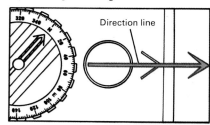

Direction line

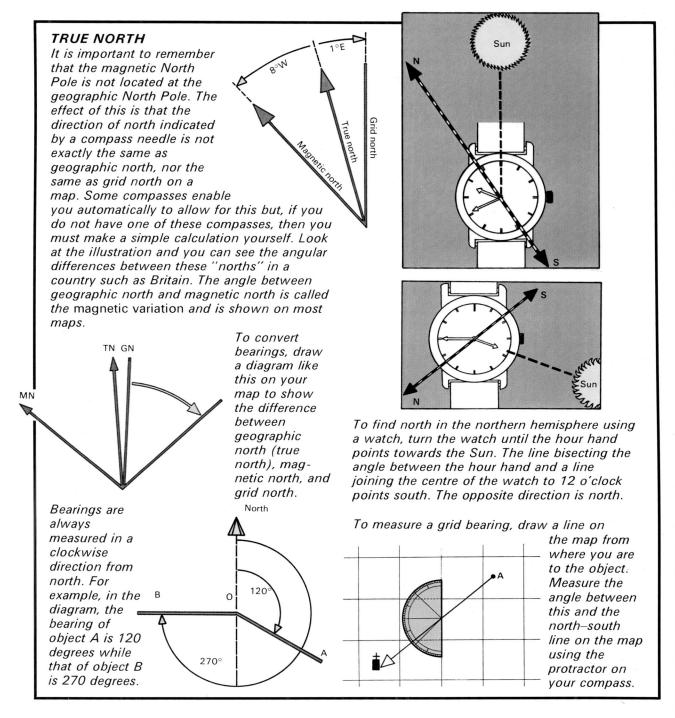

TRUE NORTH

It is important to remember that the magnetic North Pole is not located at the geographic North Pole. The effect of this is that the direction of north indicated by a compass needle is not exactly the same as geographic north, nor the same as grid north on a map. Some compasses enable you automatically to allow for this but, if you do not have one of these compasses, then you must make a simple calculation yourself. Look at the illustration and you can see the angular differences between these "norths" in a country such as Britain. The angle between geographic north and magnetic north is called *the* magnetic variation *and is shown on most maps.*

To convert bearings, draw a diagram like this on your map to show the difference between geographic north (true north), magnetic north, and grid north.

Bearings are always measured in a clockwise direction from north. For example, in the diagram, the bearing of object A is 120 degrees while that of object B is 270 degrees.

To find north in the northern hemisphere using a watch, turn the watch until the hour hand points towards the Sun. The line bisecting the angle between the hour hand and a line joining the centre of the watch to 12 o'clock points south. The opposite direction is north.

To measure a grid bearing, draw a line on the map from where you are to the object. Measure the angle between this and the north–south line on the map using the protractor on your compass.

line or road, a line of hills or a ridge. Then you can carefully line up the map with the feature you can see, and, of course, the north direction on the map will correspond with north on the ground. But remember, methods such as this can only give you *approximate* directions. If you need to find your way more accurately, for example, if you are looking for a way down off a mountain, you will still need to use a compass.

Once you have set the map, you can compare features that you can see on the ground with those marked on the map.

CHOOSING YOUR ROUTE

If you're walking along a pavement, you probably wouldn't choose deliberately to step in a pothole. The same goes for the country. Reading the land, so that it becomes almost second nature, is a useful skill to learn, especially if you are in really rugged terrain. For example, there is a mountain in Tayside in Scotland called Schiehallion. It is well over 1,000 m (3,000 ft) high but, from one side, it looks nearly conical in shape. From the road on that side, it looks as though the best way to go up the mountain is straight up the slope facing you. If you do make the ascent that way, however, you will be faced with a seemingly never-ending series of ups and downs as you are forced to deal with a large number of ridges. In fact, it is much easier to climb the mountain by a path up the apparently longer shoulder.

Use the information on the map, and your own eyes and judgement to work out the best way to get from A to B, especially if there is no obvious path. If you want to reach a particular point and there seems to be a hill in the way, try to save as much energy as possible by staying as long as you can at the same height. If you don't have to (or don't want to), there's no point in climbing to the top of the hill, only to have to come down the other side. Work your way around the hill at the same level. This is called contouring – it may mean you have to walk a little further, but it should be a lot less tiring.

Animals, such as sheep and deer, are very good at crossing country and sometimes, where they have followed the same route many times, you can make use of their tracks. But take care, these animals are very sure-footed and may be able to go where you cannot and, of course, they are probably not aiming for the same destination that you are. If you follow a track too far, you might be faced with an uncrossable river or dangerous crags.

Don't forget that water always runs downhill, and if you need to get down from high ground, it might be possible to follow a stream, especially, if you can find it on your map. But beware any boggy ground which you might find where the stream reaches lower ground.

If you're following the river to its estuary and find yourself wandering along the beach at low tide, don't lose track of how far you've walked. When the tide turns, are you sure there'll be a way out?

Here is a challenge for two walkers. They must use there skill to work out which is the best route to the top of the hill.

A stream bed may look like a footpath – sometimes useful to escape downhill but there might be crags waiting for you!

A deer track leads to better grazing near the lake – but there is boggy ground here too!

A sheep track leads to the river where animals drink – but there is no bridge!

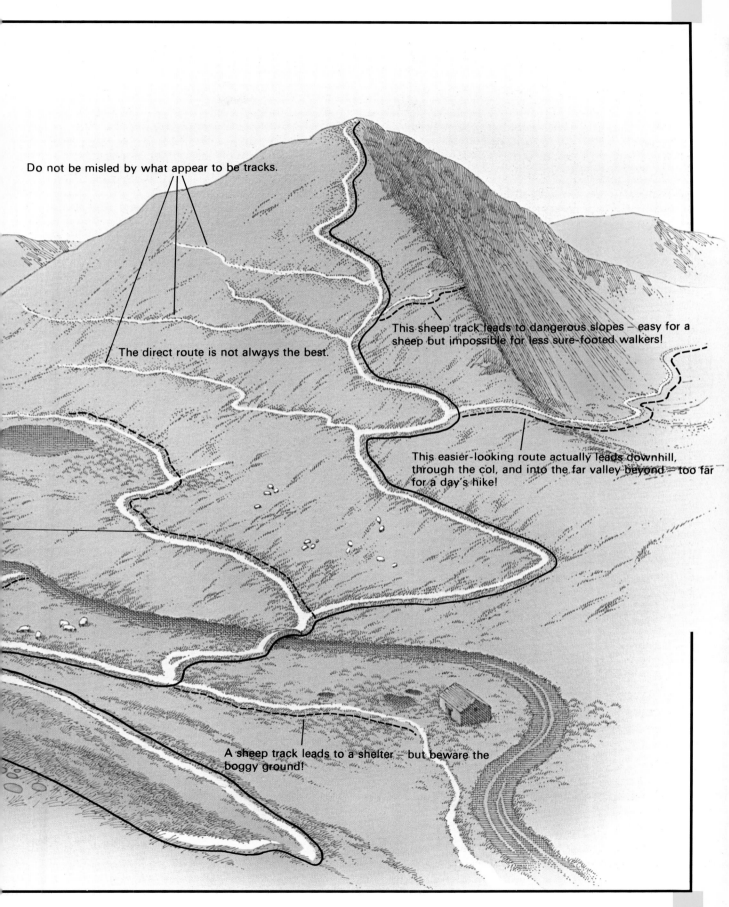

Do not be misled by what appear to be tracks.

The direct route is not always the best.

This sheep track leads to dangerous slopes – easy for a sheep but impossible for less sure-footed walkers!

This easier-looking route actually leads downhill, through the col, and into the far valley beyond – too far for a day's hike!

A sheep track leads to a shelter – but beware the boggy ground!

READING THE WEATHER

In some parts of the world, such as much of central Australia, the weather is very stable. Every day might be bright and sunny, and sometimes rain does not fall for years. Even in those areas, however, the air temperature at night may fall very sharply. In Europe, and especially Britain, the weather is notoriously changeable. The picture of the British family out for the day with waterproofs and umbrellas suggests that, even in high summer, rain showers can suddenly occur.

It's always worth checking what the weather is likely to do before you go out of doors. Even a trip to the local park can

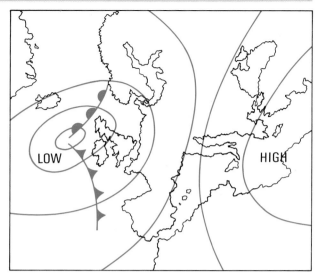

A typical weather map showing a "depression". The continuous lines are called isobars and are lines of equal air pressure. The lines with sharp triangles show the front of a mass of cold air while those with the rounded "knobs" show a mass of warm air. You can also see the centres of high and low air pressure.

These great, threatening "anvil" clouds are called cumulonimbus and they normally bring heavy rain or even thunderstorms with them.

These wispy, white clouds are called cirrus. These always suggest the arrival of warm air and, when they thicken across the sky, rain should be expected.

This is often called a "mackerel sky" and is made up of high, altocumulus clouds. Any rain from these often evaporates before it reaches the ground.

be miserable if you find, too late, that you should have taken a waterproof or an extra sweater! But, if you're planning any major trip, especially into more remote or mountainous country, it's vital to know what the weather is going to be like. Newspapers and television usually provide a national and general regional forecast for the next 24 hours and will also in-

A land devil photographed in Kenya. Note the dust raised by the narrow vortex.

dicate the likely conditions for the next few days. It's also possible to get more accurate regional forecasts through telephone services. To understand newspaper forecasts, it's useful to understand what the various terms mean. Your school or local library should have books on climate, weather, and weather forecasting which will help.

Mountain weather can be very different even from the weather which is experienced nearby. Whenever you venture into the hills, it is always worth checking the local forecast, and in many mountainous areas, there are information centres which can help. Many countries also have their own folklore or "sayings" concerning the weather. Some of these are misleading, although some, such as *red sky at night, shepherd's delight*, do stem from an accurate idea of conditions.

How to predict the weather

There are six major things to look out for when working out what kind of weather is on the way. You should check the:
1 State of the sky and clouds
2 Wind direction and speed
3 Atmospheric pressure
4 Air masses approaching
5 Temperature
6 Humidity (amount of moisture in the air)

To assess many of these, you need to be a professional forecaster and have complicated instruments. But you can certainly learn quite a lot, especially locally, from looking at the sky. And a home barometer or a pocket altimeter can tell you a lot about pressure changes.

Why not try making your own forecasts around your home by looking at cloud patterns on a daily basis?

Wind chill

This shows the effect of wind speed (expressed on the Beaufort Scale) on temperature (in degrees Centigrade). The temperatures listed on the top row are those which would be shown on a thermometer protected from any wind; those below are the equivalents at the various wind speeds. The area coloured blue represents the danger zone, in which there is risk of exposed flesh suffering frostbite. Remember that freezing point is 0°C.

Wind Force	Temperature							
	+50	+40	+30	+20	+10	0	−10	−20
2	+48	+37	+27	+16	+ 6	− 5	−15	−26
3	+40	+28	+16	+ 4	− 9	−21	−33	−46
4	+36	+22	+ 9	− 5	−18	−36	−45	−58
5	+32	+18	+ 4	−10	−25	−39	−53	−67
6	+29	+15	− 1	−17	−31	−46	−61	−77
7	+27	+11	− 4	−20	−35	−49	−67	−82
8+	+26	+10	− 6	−21	−37	−53	−69	−85

WHY LANDSCAPES ARE ALL DIFFERENT

Everywhere you go, you will see that the landscape presents a different face. And, of course, this face changes with time as the forces of weathering, erosion, and so on carry out their work. Although they can't always be seen, the rocks under the surface provide the building blocks on which the scenery we can see is moulded. And, of course, the mountain-building activities of our ever-restless planet mould these rocks into basic shapes – which in

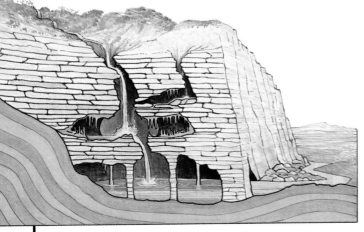

A cross-section through an area of typical limestone country.

turn are sculpted by the effects of wind, rain, rivers, frost, ice, heat, plant life, and animals (including humans).

Different kinds of rocks tend to occur in different structures and are affected in different ways by weathering and erosion. For example, limestone rock contains

mostly calcium carbonate, often in crystalline form. Rocks such as this would have been deposited originally as a lime-rich sediment at the bottom of the sea, piled in layers, one on top of the other. As the great forces, generated deep within our planet, thrust and tore at the Earth's crust, then these rocks might have been folded into troughs and crests. But one of the important features of limestone is that water can pass through it and that it is dissolved by acidic water. Consequently, a stream carving its way across limestone country may disappear underground to dissolve great cavern systems. Here stalactites and stalagmites will be found, as limestone is redeposited from dripping, lime-rich water.

A GLACIATED VALLEY

If you are fortunate enough to be walking through a valley like this, there will be a number of features that you can look out for. Sometime in its past, this valley will have been carved out by the slow movement of huge glaciers of ice. The results are easy to spot.

1 *At the head of the valley is the armchair-like area called a* cwm, corrie, *or* cirque. *Behind this, the mountains themselves have razor-edged shapes, called* arêtes, *or are carved into three-sided* pyramidal peaks.

2 *The valley itself is U-shaped and, because the ice has cut straight through it, the tributaries running into the main valley will be left as hanging valleys. The original spurs left by the meandering river will be truncated.*

3 *In the valley, there are other features typical of glaciation. For example, any rock which the ice has ground its way over, will have been moulded to look like the back of a sheep and is called a* roche moutonnée.

4 *And the melting glacier may well leave behind various piles of debris called* moraines.

Desert scenery is one which has been scorched by the sun and blasted by wind-blown sand.

pyramidal peak

arête

bergschrund

cwm

hanging valley

truncated spur

U-shaped valley

roche moutonnée

drumlins

terminal moraine

SETTING UP CAMP

There are probably as many different ideas about good and bad tents and campsites as there are people who regularly camp out. There is certainly an immense variety of shapes and sizes of tents available for different purposes. They range widely in price and are made from different materials. Some are light, some heavy, some suitable for camping in the freezing conditions of the Antarctic,

1 Ridge tents are still very popular. They can be stable, weatherproof, and roomy. They are made in a variety of sizes suitable for "base camps" or for backpacking.

2 Tunnel tents are a comparatively recent innovation. For their weight and bulk, they can be roomy inside. Some people complain that heavy snow can accumulate on them and make them sag.

3 Wedge tents were once very common for lightweight camping. Pitched end-on into the wind they are very weatherproof. Also, because they are smaller at the foot end, they are lighter and less bulky than the equivalent ridge tent.

Opposite: if you can find some suitable poles, or a wall and some stones, and you have come prepared with a lightweight groundsheet, you can easily make a temporary shelter to escape the worst of the weather.

3

4

4 *Dome-shaped tents with one or two sectional hoops for support are very roomy for their bulk and weight. Also, they offer more shoulder space for their height. Pitched properly, they are also very stable but good-quality tents of this type can be expensive to buy.*

while others are designed for use on safari where they need to be cool and insect-proof. There is even one type of tent which has been made, with a solid floor, and can be suspended from the side of mountains – occupants need to be careful when they leave it!

Take advice from magazines and from your outdoor retailers but, in the end, it will be your own experience which dictates to you the best kind of tent for your needs.

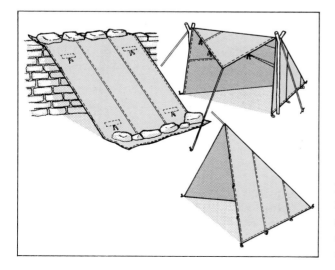

To start with, why not try a night under canvas (these days usually cotton or nylon) in your garden. Then, you need hardly spend a fortune on your first tent or you could even borrow one. Even if it rains, you can always sneak back to your warm, dry, comfortable bed! But this kind of experience does help to show you what you need from a tent.

With all the shapes and sizes available, it's hard to choose a good tent, but here are a few general guidelines. If you are going to camp where it might be cold, wet, and windy, your tent must obviously be waterproof. But, if it's completely waterproof, condensation might build up on the inside overnight and, when you move in the morning, you still get soaked! Your tent should also be stable when it's windy; tents have been known to blow away in the night, taking their occupants with them. It shouldn't flap because the noise will keep you awake. It should be fairly easy to pitch (especially useful if it's raining). It should be big enough for you and your gear and, if you are carrying it on your back, it should be light and compact.

Plenty of experience will be your best guide to selecting a good site to pitch your tent. You will probably make some mistakes at first (though hopefully, not serious ones). There are guidelines that you should follow nonetheless.

You can camp on an official campsite where there are usually various facilities, including toilets, taps, washing areas, and sometimes shops. In these places, you may be told where to pitch your tent. But, if you really want to get away from it all, then you can "camp wild". Remember, though, land usually belongs to someone so, if you think you need it, make sure you have permission to pitch your tent. Also be sure to have everything with you that you are likely to need for the length of time you are camping.

A WELL-ORDERED CAMP

In really wild country, selecting a place to pitch your tent can be very important. In the picture shown above, a modern hoop tent has been pitched in one of the wilder parts of North Wales. Despite the rocky and hilly nature of the terrain, the camper has found a spot which is reasonably flat, grassy, and free from stones. The tent has been pitched with the rear facing into the wind and it has been given extra stability by weighting it down with heavy rocks. On one side a pile of rocks provides extra shelter, but there are no overhanging cliffs or trees. There is a source of water nearby, but the tent is uphill of it so there is no danger of flooding during the night. You can see all the equipment that the camper has brought along.

At the Great Beaver Lake in Scandinavia, the solitary wanderer in the picture below has brought out his sleeping bag to air in the sunshine and is busy about his cooking. The springy turf probably made for a comfortable night. Even though the conditions may seem to be just about perfect, it is as well to be prepared. Don't pitch the tent too near the water and make sure that your tent and sleeping bag are good enough to cope with changing weather or a cold, wet night.

REMEMBER TO AVOID. . .

- pitching so that your head lies downhill;
- pitching broadside into the wind;
- pitching on undulating, rocky ground;
- pitching downhill of a river or stream;
- pitching under trees or rocks;
- pitching on wet or boggy ground;
- pitching on ground where you are unable to insert tent pegs;
- pitching near water where animals regularly drink or wallow;
- leaving any rubbish behind;
- making open fires.

SAFETY FIRST

To apply the kiss of life lie the person on the ground on his/her back. Make sure that the person's airway is clear. Kneel beside the head. Tilt the person's head back by pulling the chin upwards and the top of the head down. The victim may start breathing.

Pinch the nose shut and open the mouth. Take a full breath, place your mouth over the victim's mouth and breathe firmly into it. Repeat every four or five seconds. **Never practise on anyone, and do not use this method until you have been properly taught.**

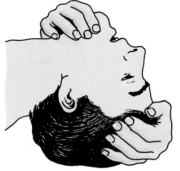
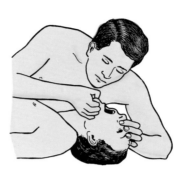
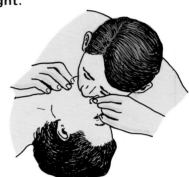

You would never cross the road without looking carefully in both directions at least once to make sure that it is clear. But it is surprising how many people venture into remote and possibly hostile countryside without the right equipment and without knowing how to cope. However experienced you are, you should never travel alone in wild country. It is better to be in a party of at least three people so that, in the event of an injury, for example, one person can go for help while one stays with the victim to keep him/her warm (or cool) and comfortable. And young people should always be accompanied by an adult if they're going into any rugged landscape.

The pictures above show some basic first-aid actions. But do not use any of them until you have been properly taught. Basically, the three most important life-threatening circumstances to look for are: is the victim breathing; is the heart functioning normally; is the victim bleeding? Broken bones come next, and then any more minor problems. At the same time, you should make sure that you and everyone else keeps calm and that neither you nor the victim is likely to be in any further danger.

Never go off on a trip into the hills, or anywhere else where there could be risk, without telling someone where you are going. At least if you have left information about your plans, then, if an emergency does occur, time is not lost in trying to find out where you were going and whether or not you have enough food to last you until the next day. Don't forget that in an emergency, a torch or whistle can be used to signal for help (six

Always carry a simple first-aid kit with you. It could contain the following items: a selection of adhesive plasters; wound dressings; stretch bandages; triangular bandages; insect repellent and bite cream; antiseptic cream; some cotton wool; a small pair of scissors; needle and thread; salt tablets and barrier cream (useful in a hot climate).

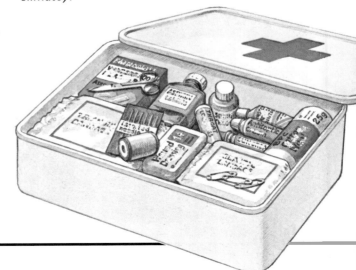

1 *You can check someone's pulse by feeling for the artery as shown.*

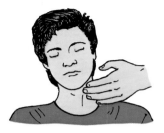

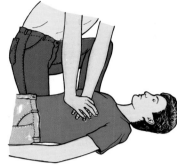

3 *The quickest way to stop bleeding is to apply firm pressure to the wound with your hand.* **Do not apply a tourniquet.**

2 *If someone's heart has stopped beating, it is possible to start it up again by heart massage.* **Never practise on anyone. Do not use this method until you have been properly taught.**

4 *This is the best position for someone to be in to recover from a serious condition. It is called the recovery position.* **Do not try to move anyone who may have damage to the back.**

long blasts on the whistle or six flashes of the torch).

It's a good idea to leave an information card with a responsible person before you set off. This is what you should include:

- Name, address, and phone number
- Responsible guardian or parent to contact
- Local address and contact
- Number of people in the party
- Time of departure and return
- Route and destinations
- Length of route
- Emergency equipment and spare food

Huddle together out of the wind for warmth.

IN AN EMERGENCY

What do you do if the worst comes to the worst, and you are stuck on a mountain with worsening weather and night falling? You should be properly prepared but remember if night falls and you can't see where you're going, stay put, if there's any danger of falling. Try to find a way to shelter from the worst of the weather.

If there's deep snow, you can protect yourself from wind chill by digging a snowhole and crawling inside. Or try sheltering from driving wind behind a wall.

Even a solitary tree can give some shade.

A TREASURE HUNT

Treasure hunts are great fun – and all the more so when played outdoors. They may take a while to organize, but it's worth it!

Each player, or each team of players, should follow a route through the countryside with the help of clues and/or a map. Ultimately, following the correct path and solving other riddles or puzzles will lead to something which has been hidden. Sometimes, nothing is hidden and it is the player who solves all the clues in the shortest possible time who is the winner.

You can organize a treasure hunt in your garden, in your local park, or in the open countryside, where it will be more exciting. You can do it just for fun or, if you are really enterprising, you can arrange a bigger treasure hunt to help raise money for charity. In any case, all treasure hunts need to be planned properly in advance.

Suppose you have chosen a suitable area about 800 metres ($\frac{1}{2}$ mile) across, and you have buried a sealed, unbreakable container of lemonade (the Holy Grail) in a safe place which no-one is likely to find accidentally. You then work out a map (which is *not* given to the players) with a route which leads to the Grail by means of clues and jumbled words. From the agreed starting point, the players are led to the first point **1** by means of a clue "In the glade of the forest stands a hermit's hut." (It is just an old fisherman's hut.) At the hut, there is a jumbled word (HENDID) and the clue to the next point: **2** Go 30 paces south-west to find the

big tree. (HENDIB)

3 Journey on across the river until you come to another river where you will find Merlin's cave. (SUNIR NI)

4 There was a jolly miller once lived by the River Teme. (DESCAR)

5 Approach with care the Lady of the Lake. She is guarded by many-headed monsters spitting poison. (In fact, three adults in hiding. They are armed with squeezy bottles filled with water and they squirt any players they see or hear.) (SLEVES)

6 See the banners fluttering in many-towered Camelot. (RABN)

The first player or team who collects and solves all the jumbled words would be able to find the Holy Grail and would be the winner of the treasure hunt. Un-scrambled, the mystery words become: "SACRED VESSEL HIDDEN BEHIND BARN IN RUINS".

Before you organize a countryside treasure hunt, there are some "golden rules" which you should follow.

1 Safety is most important at all times. (For example, do not hide clues too close to busy roads.)

2 Remember to consider other members of the public if you are not simply playing in your own house or garden.

3 Clues should be clearly visible from public areas where your are free to go.

4 Never leave any litter behind. If you are unable to go around afterwards and collect up all the clues, make sure that they are made from a material, such as paper, which will quickly decompose.

5 Animals and plants, whether wild or domestic, should never be harmed.

6 All property must be respected.

7 Follow the country code.

THROUGH THE LOOKING GLASS

Binoculars or a telescope are a real boon – they allow you to "sneak up", at least in effect, on animals, and birds, and also to bring into view pieces of countryside that you cannot reach.

There's a bewildering array of optical equipment available in the shops. But there are basic rules to follow to help you choose which are best for your needs. To some extent, you get what you pay for, and the best binoculars are usually the most expensive. But you can buy perfectly good ones quite cheaply if you know what to look for.

Firstly, you'll usually find that binoculars are described by two numbers, such as 7×50 or 10×40. The first number describes how many times the area you're looking at will be magnified. The second number describes the diameter in millimetres of the object lenses (those furthest away from your eyes when you are looking through the eyepieces of the glasses). Generally, those with the biggest object lenses will give a brighter image because they gather more light. On the other hand, they're also likely to be bigger and heavier than binoculars with smaller object lenses. Similarly, the bigger the first number, the bigger the image, but the duller it is because less light can be focused on your eyes. A 10×40 binocular is a good general-purpose type to get.

KEEPING A RECORD

Don't forget the written word. Keep a notebook handy to catalogue things that you collect, such as birds, feathers or fossils, and to make a record of your photographs. But you could even keep a full diary of how you feel and everything that happens to you when you are camping and walking. Diaries of this kind make very good reading in years to come, and they help you to take notice of what's going on around you.

WHAT YOU SEE

Birds are often small, while many other creatures may be very shy. They will run or fly to a safe distance before you get a chance to observe them if they see you first. With your binoculars, you will be able to watch wild creatures without being noticed. For example, you may be able to watch a squirrel nibbling an acorn on the other side of a pond, or birds feeding their young in their nests. You will learn a great deal about animal behaviour by observing through your binoculars.

If you can, it's best to test binoculars out of doors, in the kind of conditions in which you're likely to use them. Try to make sure that the image does not seem to "bend" at the edges of the lenses, and that you don't see a kind of rainbow effect at the sharp edges of objects. Much the same rules apply to telescopes, although magnification is usually much higher, and you'll probably need a tripod to hold a telescope steady.

CAMERAS

Look at photography books and magazines, too. It's very rewarding to have a photographic record of your outdoor adventures, or of the animals and plants that you find. Get advice on the sort of camera to buy. You can always practise by taking photographs of flowers in your garden. You may even become a professional wildlife photographer. Single-lens reflex cameras are very good for this purpose but you need to learn how to use them and they can be very expensive. There are now many, quite low-priced, and sometimes fully automatic cameras available which are virtually foolproof.

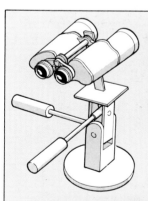

ADDED SUPPORT
For prolonged viewing with some binoculars, support is needed. Various clamps are available for use with a camera tripod.

LOOKING AT SMALL OBJECTS
A good-quality handlens or magnifying glass will make it easier to look at small creatures such as ants.

TAKING IT FURTHER

PLANTING TREES

In many parts of the world, vast areas which were once covered with forest, are now used for agriculture or for building. Trees may be blown down or they may die of old age or disease, such as Dutch elm disease. And, of course, trees are cut for timber. Much of this timber is used

for making paper pulp and is grown in plantations of conifers. But hardwood, such as mahogany, used for furniture-making and for various decorative purposes is obtained by cutting down naturally grown trees which may have taken hundreds of years to reach maturity.

You can help to preserve our countryside by joining one of the various tree-

A properly built and positioned bird-nesting box can provide a home for a family of tits, as well as being a source of interest.

Bat box

More and more birds depend upon the food that thoughtful people put out in their gardens during the winter. A bird table keeps your garden tidy and is better for the birds.

If a tree dies in your garden, and you leave it for a few years, it provides a home for all sorts of living things.

planting schemes sponsored by some of the conservation groups. That way, you can actually take part in conservation work, such as woodland management.

CHECKING FOR POLLUTION

The animal life, especially the small animals living in the muddy edges and bed of the river, will reflect the pollution level, and tell you if the water is clean. Although small, they can easily be found (if they are there). Make a small hand net of wire and curtain material of 1 mm ($\frac{1}{20}$ in) mesh, then sweep it through the mud and plants under the bank. Tip its contents into a white dish full of clear water. After a short while the indicator animals will begin to move.

LIFE IN A POND

One effect of modern living is that village ponds are now rather rare. Apart from being places to water livestock and home for the local ducks and geese, village ponds provided a habitat for all kinds of wild plants and animals. Those ponds that remain, therefore, are well worth preserving and studying.

Why not carry out a survey on a local pond and make a record of what you find there. All you need is a net and a jam jar. But, remember, once you have noted what you have caught, always put it back.

GARDENS AND WOODLANDS

Urban gardens have become ever more important havens for wildlife, as natural land is taken up for human needs. With your parents' encouragement (and permission!) you could encourage a wider variety and larger number of wild creatures to visit your own garden. Even if your garden is only quite small, or if most of it is given over to neatly trimmed lawns and perfectly laid-out flower beds with scarcely a "weed" in sight, you may be able to set aside a small part of it for wild animals. Here, you could allow the grass and other plants to grow naturally. Many different wild flowers will quickly take root. You could plant shrubs, such as buddleia, to provide food for butterflies. And, if you have a garden pond with plenty of plants, you may find tadpoles there in early spring.

NATURE TRAILS

Many countries have now set aside certain areas of the land especially for wildlife. They are usually protected from vandals and sometimes managed so that certain kinds of plants and animals can be encouraged to thrive there.

In some of these nature reserves, as they are called, trails have been laid out which you can follow. There are usually leaflets available to guide you and to tell you about the wild flowers, trees, mammals, birds, and so on that you are likely to see. Provided you stay on the trail, there should be lots to see and you will not damage the habitat. Don't forget to keep a record of your observations. It could even be useful to the reserve warden.

Index

Animals, 2, 14, 27–9
Ankle hug, 4
Arête, 18

Bearings, findings, 12–13
Binoculars, 28–9
Birds, 2, 28–30
Bleeding, stopping, 25
Boots, 6

Camera, 29
Camp, setting up, 20–1
Campsite, selecting, 22–3
Cirque, 18
Clothes, 6–7
Clouds, 16–17
Compass, 9–13
Contouring, 14
Corrie, 18
Cwm, 18

Deserts, 3, 18

First aid, 24–5
Freshwater, 3

Gardens, 31
Glaciation, 18

Keeping fit, 4–5
Knee bends, 4
  hug, 5

Land devil, 17
Life, kiss of, 24
Limestone, 18

Magnification, 28–9
Map, 10–14, 28
Maquis, 2
Moraine, 18
Mountain, 3, 18–19
  weather, 17

Nature trails, 31
North, finding, 12–13

Packs, rucksacks, 8–9
Ponds, 31

Record, keeping a, 28
Recovery position, 25
Roche moutonne, 18
Rocks, 18
Route, choosing, 14–15

Seashore, 3
Sheep path, 15
Sit-ups, 5
Sunglasses, 9

Telescope, 28–9
Tents, 20–5
  pitching, 23
Thigh shift, 5
Treasure hunt, 26–7
Tree-planting, 28–9
Triangulation, 10–11

Wall stretch, 5
Waterproofs, 7, 16
Weather, 25
  reading the, 16–17
Weather map, 18
Wind chill, 17, 25
Woodland, 2, 31

Published in 1988 by
The Hamlyn Publishing Group Limited
a division of Paul Hamlyn Publishing
Michelin House, 81 Fulham Road, London SW3 6RB

Copyright © The Hamlyn Publishing Group Limited 1988

ISBN 0 600 55739 1

Printed and bound in Italy
Front jacket illustration: John Cleare Mountain Camera, Anwar Islam,
Nature Photographers
Illustrations: John Nelson, Vince Driver, Mei Lim, Brian Delf, Eric Robson
Photographic acknowledgments: John Cleare Mountain Camera, The Photo Source
General editors: Gillian Denton, Lynne Williams